AF482022

Within

Without

Penn Inkwell

Within Without

Published in the United States of America

ISBN : 979-8-8692-5846-5

eISBN : 979-8-8692-5848-9

Foreword

Much of what's in these pages has a reason and serves a purpose.
This isn't what I would consider a journal as it's written without a
timeline it does deal with my life now and then. This is an emotional
outlet for me to vent all my emotions when the need to be released
and to not get in trouble in the process. Whether they sound good
or
bad, happy or sad, it's what was inside my head at the time. There is
an array of topics that I cover in this book, you know the usual things
love and hate, expressions, fantasy, fiction, dreams and odes to
particular people, all these subjects are covered because they
interest
me. I would consider this a type of portrait where you have to
visualize
every word written. So, enjoy what's written. When you read these
passages clear your mind and visualize everything written.
Some of these
poems are dedicated to certain people who already know who they
are.
others have dedications included with the poem.

There is a reason for being -

4got10

1000 Visions

dedicated to Heidi Voss

1000 visions come to mind,
as she searches with herself,
her visions become reality,
as she paints the canvas,
and colors spring to life,
they take shape and form,
in swirls and strokes,
the lines twist and turn then unfold,
whimsically passing over paint does create,
quite an image for many to see,
what springs forth from her head,
a goddess of art she is,
for her creations caught in time,
colors etched on a blank page,
as a reminder of her grace,
for each image of beauty captured,
many seek to escape her being,
and to create an everlasting impression,
never at a loss for ideas,
there are 1000 visions more,

Closed Eyes

I lay here in bed dreaming,
of my love for you,
and I feel the warmth of your touch,
even though you're not there,
it keeps me going through this fantasy,
though my love for you is true,
and I can never say it enough,
but I can always show you I care,
even when we're apart from each other,
and when I can't see you, your thought lingers,
sometimes in a day,
all I have to do is close my eyes,
and dream of you .... my lover,
and trace your being with my finger,
letting love show me the way,
with open or closed eye.

Fragile Entity

Dedicated to Stephanie

what emotion can make you happy,
and drive you nuts all at once,
it's the same that can shatter the mightiest,
bringing them to their knees,
it can be,
addictive,
dangerous,
exhilarating,
captivating,
deliberate in its course,
that runs straight to your core,
your heart,
LOVE,
it's never the same,
and either are you,
after you felt it's powerful spell,
leaving you weak,
delirious,
single-minded,
and wanting,
many seek to feel its rapturous touch,
they say,
it's better to love and lost,
than to never have loved at all,
LOVE,
sadness,
despair,
loneliness,
and broken,
a rollercoaster ride,

of emotions,
elation at being in love,
hatred for falling out,
LOVE the most Fragile Entity.

Peacock Mask

Dedicated to Hiedi Voss

As I entered the ballroom and search the sea,
flowing to left and right, slow dancing,
everyone swaying to music being played,
costumed in vibrant colors interacting,
mingling into this mass of humanity,
hidden before sight undercover,
some dance as they entered as a pair,
others as mischievous lovers,
they all search the floor far and wide,
waltzing from end to end, hand in hand,
there is only one I wish to be besides,
I only hope she can understand,
I only know her only by the riddle she gave,
search here about for multiple eyes,
several dull and two shining bright,
starry eyed I survey the landscape to find,
like a wolf on the hunt I spy,
in the distance beyond the mass before me,
a belle dressed in a flowing gown,
crowned in a feathered mask I see,
extending my hand for her acceptance,
for one dance is all I ask,
form my enchanting mystery before me,
hidden beauty behind a peacock mask.

Peacock Mask Unveiled

Dance With Me,
this night I want to be your partner,
graceful lady, can you not see,
I wish for no other,
was we sweep the dance floor,
from waltz to tango
Hand in hand, in rhythm and motion,
the lights above set the room aglow,
drenching the dancers in kaleidoscope colors,
every step a change in color begins,
open windows allow a summers breeze,
caused by the wind,
masked lover coupling in the shadows,
of the hall for intimacy's sake,
a kiss not viewed by prying eyes,
yet my attention returns to grace,
she before me with flirtatious being,
still veiled in feathers to hide her face,
but to unmask before the witching hour,
is forbidden in this play,
alas minutes tick slow but time well spent,
in her arms I feel free........,
dancing on a cloud up high,
above this costumed human sea,
Just You and Me Alice sings,
we are the stars in this Fantasy,
if I could take you to heaven,
that just enough for me,
the song winds the hour down,
and the time ebbs away for the end,

a ring sound out loud,
my eyes swirl about before returning again,
Silver Blue and Gold feather depart,
from and angelic face so sweet,
drawn into her eyes farther than before,
I surrender to this treat,
eyes locked upon each other,
another song Takes My Breathe Away,
a bow to my fair partner,
as we continue through the night into day.

Whisper Insanity

I whisper insanity to the wind
and she replies "liar",
again, I whisper insanity to the wind,
"Your needs must be dyer",
I've seen your sin and it's not fair
to call it insanity when it's not,
lying to all that have seen,
you know you've been caught,
whisper all you like and to whom,
your deed is done and soon the end,
you will be tied to a wall in a padded room,
without solace or friend,
misgiving and corrosion of truth,
spill forth from your mouth,
will this help your defense,
soon your soul will be heading south,
scream for all your worth,
and justify your means,
whisper insanity to the four corners,
and hide those green eyes once seen,
hang your head in shame over your deed,
repent in the lords' eyes,
no longer seeking absolution on the wind,
you whisper insanity you lie.

Battle of Dragon

With sword in hand in preparation I stand,
ready for the coming battle,
as the beast makes its descent upon me,
no, not bravery only fools rush into death,
unwavered nerves steelen my stance,
terror brought through fear by darkness.
The battle calls to all man,
though many huddle in droves like cattle,
some fight with twisted glee,
honor and pride can be fallen with but a breathe
this one must take his chance,
and through trail prove his best.
Fire rains from the sky and some run for cover,
others remain left a burnt carcass,
as evidence of the beasts might and fury,
a chance to be a knight of the day,
talons swipe forth dropping more,
blood streams from the carnage wrought about,
I draw the dragons from over,
he cannot be allowed to harm us,
this battle must cease in a hurry,
less stand with each swiping fray,
the smell of brimstone covers the air odor,
with a final thrust will victory shout........

When The Battles Over

Ever still lays Fendrel the warrior,
who did stand his ground,
against the mighty beast that laid waste,
above and to all around,
a river of red gushes from his wound,
punctured in battle was his being,
as a talon ripped into him,
a clash of man and beast defeating,
one another for reasons of their own,
for honor and glory, he fought,
to save his kin from the slaughter,
to defend life he was taught,
smoke, fire, and ruin laid about,
the stench of bodies strewn the land,
the descent of the dragon complete,
today Fendrel stood a man,
the dragon battled to claim our land as his,
many did fight now rested to the light,
the horror etched upon those witness,
to the destruction of this fight,

She was my rose,

and I loved her so,
her soft supple bud
blossoming with my touch,

a sweet rose, without thorns,
a smooth slender body,
so firm and fresh,
nearly able to stand alone,

and as she grew,
my love would feed her,
kissing each petal once,
to remind her each day,

soon she came into bloom,
with wide-eyed fascination,
living each day of life,
nourishing her existence,

then she grew thorns,
it hurt to touch her,
she withdrew from my light,
her bloom became another's,

my rose was no longer mine,
turning away from me,
a little more each day,
until she was whisked away,

now I see my rose,
withered and grey,

she is no longer the same,
she clings to life though,

begging for more,
but shadowed from the light,
I can only watch now
she was my rose

Not From

Number 2 in this Trilogy

Speak not from your lips,
for your mind has thought it,
Speak not from your heart,
for your love is untrue,
Speak not from your soul,
for you do not know the word,
Speak in silence only,
for your words are lies,
your voice at one time did send me,
but now it sounds like scratching,
once you touch did leave me weak,
but now only disgusts me,
to be in your embrace left me feeling for naught,
now I can't imagine the thought,
you learned to lie when I wasn't looking,
and played me for a fool with our friends watching,
speak not to me for you don't have a right,
now that I can't stand to see your sight.

I Cleaned Myself

I cleaned myself,
at least my emotions,
deadened emotions with no use,
pent up anger I can't vent anymore,
disgust at your love,
hatred toward you from me.
denial of your existence,
words with venom,
waiting for the moment to strike,
love doesn't live here anymore,
at least not with you,
my feeling for you changed,
while you were gone,
I found peace of mind,
something I didn't have with you,
no more I need,
no more I want,
no more give me,
no scratches along the chalkboard,
your voice silenced to my ears
the sound of sanity resides,
where my emotions once ran wild,
I would do anything for you,
but that wasn't enough,
I gave you my love,
and you spit in my face,
now I stand alone,
awaiting the next game.

Haunters Eternal Kiss (1)

Fair Belladonna, I cannot wait much longer,
Your beauty haunts me like no other,
As the evening approaches and darkness falls,
I prepare for the nights call,
Soon you will be forever mine,
With one kiss under moonshine,
I smell your scent so close,
only matched by that of a rose,
I hear the rush of blood throughout your body,
your hearts beat so haunting,
Anticipation leaves me nervous for once in my life,
Waiting for this moment with you to arrive,
I see your skin caressed by moonlight,
As you venture out into the night,
We meet on the street and chat a bit,
In our walk we find a place to sit,
My nerves wrack with fear,
I usually never act like this my dear,
But you are the woman that I seek,
To be with me in my forever sleep,
As I lean in for a prelude for a kiss,
Forever have I known the risks,
Soft, warm lips caress my cold flesh,
From lips to cheek, it is your neck I wish,
Belladonna my love with one bite,
You will share with me a new life,
I drink your essence warm of your red flood,
Leaving you laying from loss of blood,

Belladonnas Rejection (2)

Belladonna daughter of the night
sired by Haunter under the moonlight,
forever cursed under light of the sun,
no longer to live life's fun,
hatred flows through her veins,
for the one whose left her this pain,
daggers of words thrown at him,
with such intensity by her spit,
No she is not content to be render asunder.
dead to the world she once loved... no longer,
no family that's all gone, for her the mourn,
though she's not gone ....only reborn,
soulless so they say, but hatred is a emotion,
her only wish is Haunter's retribution,
remnance of life slowly fade away,
for her there is no more today,
Her first days she curses Haunter repeatedly,
for his love is this betrayal..... is cowardly,
they had been friends while she lived unaware,
for this is one secret he would not tell much less bare,
she will suffer his love for an eternity,
now that this darkness is her reality,
I know what I speak as I watch over her,
as her mind tries to cope with the only cure,
She was a child of life and lived it all,
cherishing the sun and her sister who still calls,
Belladonna hears the wind whisper her name,
but she is no longer that same.
she cannot answer for fear of fright,
all that she loved is now gone fading from her sight,
with her walks Forgotten into each night,

to keep her safe from the evil of light,
Still, she screams for Haunter's Head.
she wants his bloody corpse dead again.

Lock Inside

Part 1 of 2

locked inside your love, it is my comfort zone,
I feel always wanted here when I'm alone,
It cheers me up when I'm sad,
and brings a smile I might not have ever had,
you are the one I hold to my heart..... close,
you are my life's bouquet rose,
yet I feel you near me inside my heart,
and I know your spirit will never part,
no matter where I am thinking of you now,
I feel your love raining down on my frown,
and a smile on my face with a giggle in my voice,
knowing that you left without choice,
I live as a reminder of you ....us,
together in life as friends in trust,
now I can only hold your memory dear,
that much I my mind is clear,
but if you're watching me up above,
know that forever you hold my love,
until next we meet each other and see,
in my heart is where I'll be locked inside.

Unlocked Outside

My mortal life at an end, my soul released,
I know this is of small comfort to you I see,
I could not control the actions of another,
Even though in God's life we're sisters and brothers,
My soul no longer to this plane, bound,
Now in union with that sweet sound,
I hear an angel sing me a melody of love,
Telling me I must leave to St. Peters Gate above,
where he will judge me worthy or not to enter,
The pearly gates of heaven, loves center.
My time here has ended and I'm being called home,
In the skies of blue and the clouds beyond I will roam,
Where I will be taught what I need to get my wings,
And maybe as an angel learn so sweetly to sing,
My time now won't be fleeting as it doesn't exist,
though my memories of my friends will persist,
My love for all living things both creature and man,
grows without bound for now I understand his plan,
Don't worry I'll always look down to see you,
And to make sure you've moved on in life too,
Sometimes you'll feel me but not see, you will know,
Other times I'll be in your conscious soul,
My spirit, I feel you still hold dear,
Your prayers for me are well heard clear,
I hear you remember me as I do you.... in loving memory,
One day a guardian angel for you I can be,
Though in your memory I'm locked inside,
Now that my spirit is unlocked outside.

The Medallyon Fields

Dedicated to Cathy Coles

a lush green meadow with rolling green grass,
a place for forgetting time and letting it pass,
rows of wild flowers shone brightly in the sun,
across the landscape all colors of plants not to be out done,
flowing like a sea on land as the wind moves through them,
the sound of the sweetness vibrated through the sun stems,
looking sky ward and watching pink tinted fluffy clouds,
never once today being in doubt,
the wind so warm in its even breeze,
the sun poking out from behind the clouds in tease,
walking the meadow she saw many wonders,
each making her stop to ponder,
as a smile crossed her face so innocent,
she was genuinely happy at this moment,
she found a place to sit under and collect her thoughts,
realizing what this book had brought,
sitting under a huge oak tree giving shade,
watching the birds in the sky parade,
wings spread out gliding along the blue fairway,
thinking to herself what a way to spend the day,
staring up in the warm sun lit sky,
she thought to herself why ask why,
as she listened to the sounds,
from all these wonderous creature around,
it's such beautiful place why fight,
the fact I could be lost hmmm....... I just might,

First Date

This is how Felt when I met one Young Lady

Since we first met my heart you stole,
yet we are still apart and I stand alone,
For you belong to another,
and as I am I can only wonder,
Does he treat you like a queen,
or does he treat you cruel and mean,
Our eyes have met in passing glance,
but I always see a small chance,
Do you see I care for you,
and am willing to pay my dues,
All's fair in love and war,
anything for the one I adore,
How long will you be before you see,
for I wait as one for you my sweet,
In silence my heart breaks and weeps,
to turn fantasy into reality,
I wish for you to be by my side,
now till the end of time,
How much longer must I wait,
for us to have our first date.

Speak Write

Often I write when I can't speak,
I put my thoughts in colored ink,
so maybe I'll be able to render,
what my heart feels and to surrender,
all thoughts and doubt in her presence,
with my voice and no resentment,
of my delivery of these words, I wish to say,
maybe soon, maybe one day.
Until then I speak freely with pen,
and remain in silent with my intent,
searching for strength and will,
to speak to her before me still,
each gaze from her robs my tongue,
my mind reels and comes undone,
safety first in written solace I do find,
secondly in vocal to call her name in rhyme,
will she turn away from my words,
will eloquence and grace leave her perturbed,
so again, in fear I return pen in hand,
and scribe a note of affection from this man.

Thinking Of You

I've been thinking of you,
and I don't know what to do,
every time I close my eyes I see,
your face keeps haunting me in my dreams,
your eyes so vibrant and clear,
I can see your reflection like in a mirror,
I can be without a thought and there you are,
in my mind awake or asleep your never far,
you are a living ghost that won't let me be,
I want you to be mine so I can be at peace,
to hold you every day just a little while more,
to kiss you, prove my love for the one I adore,
to lay next to you and hold you in sleep,
never allowing you to shed a tear and weep,
I'll shower you each day with love and joy,
if only you would stop being so coy,
grant my wish and make my dream a reality,
stop leaving me an empty fantasy,
I can't bear to be this close it's unfair,
from the one I love and care,
you haunt me when I least expect it,
and leave me lonely in resentment,
I've told you of my feelings to be true,
you know I've been thinking of you..........

Suffering

I'm suffering not from a drug,
but from a woman's love,
it sends me to the highest highs,
with no end in sight,
not that I would want this to end,
this is my love and my friend,
she gives to me her strength,
and I remove her pain,
so, she can feel the joy in my heart,
that she has brought in part,
my soul for her I share,
eternally I send her my care,
I pray for no end to this romance,
I'm willing to take any chance,
to keep her by my side,
till the end of time,
embraced in passion for all to see,
whenever that may be,
god willing to keep this love so right,
by blessing this union with heaven's light,
yes I am suffering,
in this happily.

Hearts Thief

I gave you my love tried and true,
I whispered your name as the wind blew,
To carry your name to the earths end,
Only then to hear the wind repeat your name again,
Without hesitation my love to you I beset,
Never with an ounce of regret,
I strove to feel your touch,
And to hear your voice as much,
My vision of love remains only you,
And to you I pay my dues,
Therein lays my dilemma that has arisen,
My love for you has become unto me a prison,
You gave your love to another in spite of me,
I know not why or how this could seem to be,
Yet you look away from me with downcast eyes,
No words need be spoken to lie..........,
I gave you my love tried and true,
Now I see the real you,
From the pain I feel - to my heart's relief,
Someone I once love I now consider a thief.

My Wish Never-ending

my wish is to give you my love never-ending,
throughout these ages for infinity,
etched in time and sung upon the wind,
from the close reach of my arms,
to my hearts infinite grasp,
holding you close in thought,
cherishing the warmth of your presence,
always showing you the reason for my love,
without misgiving or stray thought,
to be with you day and night,
without missing one beat,
giving you a piece of my heart,
and all my soul for you to hold,
knowing the love, I have for you,
never to leave the other shelter,
finding my one true love,
never-ending.

Everything for you

Life means nothing when you are not here,
My heart doesn't beat the same without you near,
Everything I do is for you to see,
Just how much your love means to me,
You light up my life in such a way,
When you are away from me my world is grey,
I cannot live without your love,
My heart, my soul can't be without your touch,
Within your love I find everlasting pleasure,
That none can render..... let alone measure,
From these words I write
Can you see you are my life.
I pour my love into all I do,
For your happiness is my due,
To see you giggle and smile,
Makes it worth all the while,
There is nothing I won't do for you,
For my love is true,
I give you all I can give and nothing more,
For my love......... it is you I adore.
Never to stray from your heart,
I will always be there to do my part,
To hold you safe from harm,
Embraced in my arms,

Silence Of One Heart

to Diana

I find,
as I walk the line,
between friend and lover,
there is much to ponder,
do I dare risk,
our relationship,
or remain silent,
with the knowledge of my intent,
I must wonder,
if one day we would be together.

Desperate Love

when the perfect love comes to an end

What more can I say or do,
to keep from losing you,
I would get down on me knees,
if that's what you please,
But I ask you to reconsider,
don't leave me like this..... bitter,
Don't walk out that door,
I can give so much more........,
Do I mean so much to you,
that I would be abused,
I thought our love could carry us through,
to keep us from being untrue,
Did I guess of us wrong,
to think our love would last long,
Please stay at least for one more day,
there's got to be another way,
Is there no way to salvage this relationship,
I would try at all cost and risks,
For the sake of our love,
before it's all said and done.

Moments Before

Have I wasted my love for you,
was there someone else in you untrue,
That you would leave me alone to stand,
without reason to your cruel brand,
Wasted for all because you didn't care,
you pined for someone new, that's not fair,
How would you expect me to understand and deal,
I gave and you took without being real,
My love on you wasted, my time with you wasted,
my patience for all you put me through tested,
I could have be with someone that wanted me,
someone whose heart I could please,
I gave you my love without vain,
and you leave me to suffer heart break and pain,
Through thick and thin we'd weather,
now you run to another for shelter,
yet you still walk for the door,
in your haste to leave my love on the floor,
now leave me be..........

Two Roses

the first rose I give to you is white,
it signifies our friendship,
and my gratitude for your equality,
in both giving and receiving,
and knowing friendship isn't one way,
and holding confidence in one another,
being there to help me know what's right,
helping me when I fall and trip,
and not condemning my skewed reality,
for being there always believing,
even when I loose my grasp in the day,
or sharing laughter and sorrow with each other,
the second rose I give to you blue,
this if one that I've given to a choice few,
this represents my highest bid of confidence,
trusting you completely without reservance,
this friendship has passed into something special,
and in my life that is very pivotal,
to know someone will believe in me always,
to help stay my course and not stray,
giving reassurance when things get bad,
for that I'm forever grateful and glad,
two roses one white ....
two roses one blue ....

Then Comes Dawn

Like the night wind is her caress,
cool and light to the touch,
long flowing mane adores her face,
gazing into her eyes is like the moon,
a mystery there in lies deep,
sun covered skin aglow,
her girlish laughter carries on forever,
singing on the unseen wind,
She very much is a welcome guest.
Thinking about her leaves this one a mess,
to be away from someone like this,
my awkwardness leaves much in doubt,
though in truth I feel with her in tune,
as I slumber, and the sun creeps,
visions dance in my mind to know,
always in dream I surrender,
and for but moments I win,
and she accepts my hands request.
Only then comes Dawn.............

My Genie

My happiness was from you,
and to you I give my love true,
You gave to me like so few,
when no one else was around,
You lifted me of the ground,
so, I won't have to frown,
You gave my life reason to exist,
when this seeming death did persist,
In this darkness I could not resist,
when I was overwhelmed by loneliness,
you showed me loves happiness,
and the joy of bliss,
for your spark of light so beautiful,
For that I am always grateful,
you never once judged me cruel,
On this occasion I'll forever cherish,
till the day my love does perish,
This is my final wish,
In my heart I still hold your love.

My Hope

Once I had hope and life was good,
but then for some reason she left me alone,
maybe I cared for her more than she for me,
she was indeed a stunning view,
long wavy black hair down to her waist,
green eyes to bring a man to his knees,
a vibrant warm and beautiful smile
with a girlish giggle and laugh,
waifish of figure but full to hold,
dark skin and long legs end the view,
but she was entertaining and versed,
willing to talk in conversation and I would listen,
which struck me as odd for a bit,
that I was attracted to what laid within,
a soul of grace and charm,
very sweet and warming,
this is what trapped me,
to this unknowing beauty who caught me,
as we became what I thought close,
I could read her mind and finish her words,
she would giggle and tell me,
how can you do that,
I could only say maybe it's meant to be,
I would have done anything for her,
but it was for naught,
she soon disappeared from my view,
without a word, without a trace,
leaving me haunted by her face,
I once thought I had Hope...........

Tanya

I write these words that they may touch your soul,
like that which you have never known,
to caress your being and hold you enthralled,
captivated by these words that call,
I've watched you age with time,
through these eyes of mine,
so close and yet so far,
I can hear the beat of your heart,
through your eyes I have seen the reflection,
of that which is the attraction,
I've seen the innocence of your soul,
though I don't know if it's for me to behold,
I've seen the aura of your being,
so warm and gentle........comforting,
beauty shown upon your face,
is that of your inner grace,
eyes shining, sparkling, ...so vibrant,
giving forth bright radiance,
a smile that haunts the mind's eye,
showing me your other side,
a subtle charm added to your soul everlasting,
captivating sweet never-ending.

SARAH

Your vision does tend to send me,
when I stand before your beauty,
And begin to see your charms and grace,
my mind wonders to another place,
Though here I stand witness to your display,
as you dance through the day in your way,
Light blue eyes intense and erotic,
inviting to dare a risk,
Long flaxen hair in thickened mane,
cascading gently about your defined face,
Skin so soft to the touch like lace,
a disarming smile to leave you tame,
A nymph carefree and pretty as she please,
with a touch like a summers breeze,
Did I mention sharp of words and wit,
all qualities that make you hard to resist,
Truly a sight of beauty to be held,
my heart for you would melt,
I admit here that I have feeling for you,
deeply buried though you have seen a clue,
I've held you close in my arms embrace,
but only as a friend for sake of face,
Though by now I keep my heart in detention,
when I'm around your notice and attention,
For me to say what's on my mind,
would be out of line and not be right,
Sometimes the words fall short of rhyme,
but I found the words this time.
Even now my revealing you still won't be mine.

Written for Another

Whenever you are away,
I'm always thinking of you.
No matter how far apart,
my heart will remain true.
Despite the distance,
that has come between us.
I will forever love you,
just as much.
So, no matter where you are,
hold me close to your heart.

Forgotten

I'm there when no one else is,
In your times of sorrow and need,
To offer comfort even if by second,
I'm not who you chose to cry upon,
And yet you find your way to me,
I will try to ease your pain,
And bring a smile to your face,
Only for you to leave without thanks,
I am who you pour your heart to,
I have seen your very soul,
I've helped you survive your tragedies,
And nurse your battered spirit and wound,
Without so much of a glance your gone,
My purpose in your life served,
I am no longer need by you,
I am your friend or so you say,
Yet you won't give me the time of day,
Second hand in your life,
I am, until needed forgotten.

How odd that you won't return the favor...........

Free-Flow

here, there, everywhere,
perplexed yet,
free-flow through it all,
got it,
liquid thought, maybe lucid,
not concrete, but yet,
keep on moving,
up, down all around,
here, there, somewhere,
come and go, leave and stay,
like a shot from nowhere,
free-flow into nothing,
something, anything come on,
jump into another space,
but stay where you are,
just move through time,
I'm where I want to be,
in your world out of mine,
enter the mind, leave the mouth,
words of wisdom, words of fools,
soar high above the clouds,
like a bird on the winds,
ignite the fire within got it,
got it just flow, free fall,
I'm free be free

My Prayer

Can you help me find the light,
help me find the path that's right,
so that I may live and prosper,
that I may grow and be proper,
to bask in his glow,
as many have done long ago,
to bathe in his bright radiance,
and to seek his counsel and guidance,
I believe in the Lord as always,
my faith is strong as i try not to stray,
but sometimes I need a hand,
from a kind soul who understands,
my name is written in the book,
that St. Peter uses to look,
I am born one of the flocks,
though in my way I'm lost,
I do worship in my own way,
for he sees my every day,

Written Thoughts

As ink flows from my pen,
to write thoughts that come from my head,
sometimes it weird to see,
what's going on up there in my reality,
I write whatever comes to mind,
good or bad at least I tried,
venting my frustrations in ink,
as thoughts come to think,
though I will admit even I,
can't write all the time,
every so often I struggle with words,
that won't flow well at first,
some days a blank page,
stays that way ....unchanged,
other days i write like a river flow,
not knowing when I'll run cold,
it's a course I'm following,
it's just I don't know when it'll be ending.
as ink flows onto the paper with my pen moving,
sentences begin to form from my writing,
what I'm thinking about becomes a reality,
even if it is just a fantasy.

Misjudged Book

You judged this book by its cover,
and you found out late to discover,
things are not what they seem,
much like when you sleep and dream,
you said some very wrong things,
and truth to tell they did sting,
by my appearance you said you dread,
the thought of my being was a threat,
but in time you read between the lines,
and our friendship to you became a delight,
I never turned my back on you,
that much was very true,
but now your gone from my life,
and I am reminded by sight,
memories of the past that leads us here,
to a friend I now hold very dear,
I'm glad you misjudged this book,
you learned it wasn't all in the look,
I still value our friendship even though,
after all this time it shows,
even after all that's changed
your name and face still remain,
etched in the pages of this ones soul,
as a valued lesson to be told.

Long Gone

Long gone are you,
how long has it been,
since you left in such a rush,
without a trace to trail.
This is so true,
your name now rides the wind,
leaving only dust,
how could you have been so frail.
Behind you left much sorrow,
those still in wonder,
reeling from the shock set in,
you imposed on them.
I will wake up tomorrow,
and stop to ponder,
what happen to you within,
my thoughts to you i send.
I often stop to think,
your still here,
imagining you voice and laughter,
then remembering your depart.
I would have tried to stop your sink,
but I didn't hear,
this just leaves me madder,
and life hard.

Personal Belief

If I follow my desire and try,
at least to my heart I did not lie,
In this my challenge in life,
for all that I can be I must fight,
For all I hope to Achieve,
this is as I believe,
In myself I must be true,
so that one day someday soon,
All will be within my reach,
for each challenge that I defeat,
I will not compromise my principle,
just for someone else's approval,
I must go my own way,
hoping never to stray,
To Succeed and Achieve.

Live And Learn

As I look back on my life,
and see the mistakes I've made,
just like everyone else has,
but hey live and learn right,
experience they say is the best teacher,
learn from your mistakes,
strive to make yourself better,
whether people see that I've learned,
that's their option or ignorance,
I'm prone to error like everyone else,
maybe then they see,
there's no one better than me,
at living my own life my own way,
even when they don't let you live your life,
they close the doors you open,
denying you the right that is yours,
to live and learn as best you can,
making your way through this world,
to use what you've learned,
and to stand on your own,
since life is not a game,
but a teacher.

Reality

Wonder at life's endless possibilities,
of just what could happen by talking,
communicate to someone ....
talk to him, talk to her, talk to anyone,
anything in life can happen,
if in life you do partake in.
In the blink of an eye,
open the door say hello say goodbye,
endlessness streams infinitely,
altering every turn in your reality,
it leaves you the choice,
at this aspect I say rejoice.
Through vocals and signs,
find common design,
it's all within your hand,
it's yours understand,
opportunity lay in wait.... abound,
endless reality all around.

January

January the start of a new year,
for the past pause but a moment and shed a tear,
This day brings forth a year of new,
and lord knows many have paid their dues,
But through trials and tribulations,
I've come to the realization,
That even though I am here to be,
it's through clear eyes I cannot see,
For reasons of life, I often ponder,
why we stop to wonder,
Go........ move an inch forward,
one wrong move sends us a mile backward,
Stop often renders us null and void,
it's a catch 22 .... some choice,
With each new year's tiding,
and each old season in hiding,
May a box unlike Pandora's,
smile happily upon us,
Old vibrations of the past give way,
as the bell toll for a brighter day,
With outstretched arms I stand,
searching for a glimmer to understand,
As time slowly slips away to this new year,
there isn't much to fear,
What goes up must come down,
in a constant circle all around,

Just Another New Useful Attempt Requiring You

Mind Spring

I was having a dream, lost in between, fantasy and reality,
I was tossing and turning, my mind was churning,
With visions of a sweet lady, quite a treat,
I know it sounds crazy, I close my eyes and repeat,
The dreams are always different, some I'd like to repent,
So close and yet far but still adjacent, leaving me spent,
I can feel your touch, but I feel it's a sin,
Knowing that much, to return the feelings within,
I've seen her many times, her vision clouds my mind,
To hear her on the winds chime, drawing to my treasure find,
I battle to win this struggle each night, time is against me,
But my mind thinks it's right, to dream an eternity,
Only to leave me alone when I wake, then to haunt me in lay,
How do you make a getaway, knowing your mind will betray,
With hyperions time in wane, the rem cycle completing sleep,
I leave this slumber plane, returning awake in disbelief,
The mind can play tricks on you, even when you just want peace,
And often leaves you the fool, as you surrender your leash,
To all that's real, in this reality,
and your mind deals, only the fantasy.

Only Human

No matter what I seem to hold,
It's never that pot of gold,
This cloud with no silver lining,
Rains on my parade and my findings,
As fast as things start, they grind to a halt,
Sometimes it feels like all my fault,
I try to do what's right,
But a shroud befalls my sight,
When I try to reach for the stars,
I find that I'm too far,
Life seems to find a way to prolong,
My suffering right or wrong,
I wish I could find a way,
To a better day,
But instead, I find another wall,
I try again hoping I won't fall,
Luck, fate, destiny, they all make their plays,
Moving my goals farther away,
Now I don't know what to do,
People still tell me I have much to lose,
If they could help, I wish they would,
If they can, some don't when they should,
I know I have a purpose in life,
It's just that I can't seem to find,
I stand one among the rest,
Only hoping for the best.

Change

In this day and age,
I find that everything goes through change,
At least of some kind,
Just a faint memory to remind,
Almost but not quite the way it used to be,
All you have to do is look around and see,
Look at the grass and the trees,
The winds sing in its breeze,
The sun rises and set the same,
but still, there's change,
As time goes by and days become years,
change is always moving gear,
broken down streets pave the way,
the kids grow from the games they play,
Flesh and blood become ashes,
As we move through these passages,
Time doesn't change if you're wondering,
Us, we do all the changing,
In everyday and in everything we do,
We're always looking and leaving clues,
There's always something there to remind me,
Of what was there........ what used to be,
As far and wide as the eye can see,
Wonders to behold in reality.

Cycles

So many places and friends in time,
a circle about you takes five again,
for the times and life's, you will always see,
familiar traces of the past in their faces,
unlocking memories of your ancient path,
each connection has reason and rhyme,
as you meet up again......... friends,
the familiarity to each just seems to be,
drawn by some strange sense that retraces,
repeatedly speaking in signs that last,
Feelings of remembrance come about you,
with these encounters that brings you to ponder,
why these people seem to fit,
into your life much like a puzzle,
your mind tries to recall,
seeking out that which you know is true,
different but still the same you wonder,
through your minds haze is the wall you hit,
you don't understand but there's no trouble,
as you venture down the darken halls,
In sleep the past awakens to reveal you,
as you were as you are and will be,
and still, you notices the five same,
from every stage in life the act continues,
until you find reason to the madness,
first you were born into the past then returned anew,
for reasons of his own you returned to see,
to learn more again and try to change,
that is unless you already paid your dues,
in which case you are truly blessed.

Emote

Words can't describe,
what I'm feeling inside,
neither happy nor sad,
far be it that I'm mad.
It's an emotional state,
which at times you can relate,
i find myself calm and at ease ....
something like peace.
Yet not the same,
in the middle my emotions remain,
all in check like water behind a dam,
I just am.......

Dreamscape

As I enter this night dream state,
you are there,
waiting for me to sleep,
to haunt me in my dreams,
It's a twist of fate,
that someone so fair,
would be mine to keep,
for an eternity it seems,
In our time I share all of me with you,
even knowing soon I will awake,
feeling your passion seems real,
knowing I hear no sound when you speak,
All that I am is true,
my wish is my mistake,
but that is mine to deal,
for this realm I will soon leave,
Though I awaken from my haze,
I can no longer see your stare,
It is you that I seek,
so it can be more than a dream,
I've been thinking of you of late,
hoping to be part of a pair,
the two of us my sweet,
if destiny would deem fair.

Visions

I see when I am sleep, through closed eyes I see all,
thoughts and dreams, hold me enthralled,
I hear and see, just like the day,
ghastly vision haunts me in no way,
I see images from past and present,
sometimes yours, sometimes mine granted,
A fortune to be told as only I can see,
whether it be truly reality or fantasy,
Seeing through the mist that clouds your eyes,
peering through the thickened veils mine do pry,
Forms taking shape some of beast, others of man,
the visions I see I understand,
The tales woven in lucidity,
a dream of reality,
Beneficial for both you and me,
only if you heed my tale see...
Be aware that dreams are real,
they hold clues to this day deal,
yet in-between this does my mind partake.
I dream when I'm asleep, I see when I'm awake,

Out of Body

On this occasion when I did lay to sleep,
I dreamt my soul did release from my body's' keep,
As I roamed through my house,
Passing through brick and wood silent as a mouse,
Outside I ventured in the night sky,
Up near the moon and stars in twilight,
I did hear my name called from a distance,
I followed the ring of sound by chance,
And found a friend in distress,
Without thinking I entered the hall to a witness,
There she stood in her pjs and shock,
She said "What are you doing here" I caught,
My reply was you called me and I came,
she reached to touch me unlike a dream I remained,
We talked about her plight in waking life,
With the end she did thank me for bearing her strife,
And I left for home but not before exploring,
the wonders of not being bound is quite exhilarating,
By tetter I returned safely to wake very tired,
Knowing I did not sleep only my body did retire,
Going to school with remembering a recent past,
She came to say " I something strange to ask",
In detail hers emerged to match mine,
I told her I might be a fluke this one time,
this reassurance did comfort her mind,
But our shared adventure left her to deny,
call it what you will astral projection or magic,
It's a reality take your pick.................

Reincarnation

Return to life from the cusp,
just as you have times before,
enter the stage from the beginning,
your soul is disguised once more,
Imprisoned within flesh and blood,
as the clock ticks on borrowed time,
your mission forgets the past,
and continue to grow in life you find,
Your soul pulls in directions,
strangely familiar with slight hesitations,
you've been here before it's true,
Deja vu from past connections,
As the soul learns anew,
and you come closer to the end,
with wisdom learned through trails due,
will reincarnation be needed again,
Have you learned the way,
and enter the higher plane,
or return to the path
and remain the same.

Tainted Souls

Dedicated To Everyone on Earth

Tainted souls are we all by choice you see,
given free will as an option to be,
take your pick of things that present themselves,
and chose what you do and just as well,
the line of black and white has long been blurred,
souls of black know their role as white does sure,
but those that dance on the razor watch well keep,
delving into both good and evil deep,
equal the sum of both parts by purgatory linen,
tainted through life to do what's wrong or right,
walk into the dark or into the light,
some strive for the better other no so done,
often willing to play games to be the one,
in life we pay for past deeds committed long ago,
you work to clean the slate for what you chose,
heaven and hell will wind the time for your arrival,
watching for both praise and sin in this your trial,
enter heaven's gate clear and clean a soul,
or into hells brimstone stench the bells toll,
either way we are all tainted souls.

Unto Myself Strange

when the mirror lied

Sometimes it's not me,
I wake up there and see,
It's someone else………. it has to be,
Hollowed eyes devoid of emotions,
Empty of soul, no reflection,
But I still see a connection,
A hint of great uncertainty flashes,
Across this images' face which crashes,
This moment of Sur reality and lucidity clashes,
Searching for something that is not clear,
It attempts to breach the separating mirror,
Staring back at me with an uneasy fear,
I felt the pain of rejection set in,
Brought about by this mirrored image of sin,
There is no love, or life within,
And it begins to transform a change,
Yet the image of me ………does remain,
This is what I've become unto myself strange.